5 MINUTES A DAY TO LIVING BEYOND RICH

~~~~~~

The Easy, Simple, Blunt, No Nonsense Personal Finance Guide for Busy People

By
Jen McDonough

PUBLISHED BY 3D PUBLISHING

5 Minutes a Day to Living Beyond Rich by Jen McDonough

Copyright © 2013 by Jen McDonough

Published in 2013 by 3D Publishing

Book ISBN -13: 978-0984770441

Book ISBN-10: 0984770445

Electronic ISBN-13: 978-0-9847704-5-8

Electronic ISBN-10: 09847704053

3D Publishing, Lindstrom, MN

FOREWORD

Would you take action to find financial freedom, peace, and joy if you only had to spend 5 minutes a day on your finances? Would you invest 300 seconds of your day to reduce financial stress in your life?

If you answered yes to the above questions, I say kudos to you for taking action to read this book!

Carving time out of your schedule to further educate yourself on something that has the potential to change your life will be rewarding! You get 'double brownie points' especially since:

- **Personal finance can be a very boring subject to learn about.**

- **Personal finance is not talked about openly in our society (it is like discussing one's underwear in public).**

Being that personal finances is a hush, hush subject in our society, it probably explains why many people today are living in such pain, embarrassment and shame around their finances.

It seems strange when you step back to think about the incredible impact finances can have on our lives, our community, and our work. Yet knowing this, we still don't talk about it, we don't take time to learn about it, and frankly, the thought of doing so can give many of us the shiver me timbers.

Why do I know all this?

I use to be one of "those people" who:

- Didn't talk about my finances.

- Didn't have time to learn how finances worked.

- Didn't have any inclination to learn about finances. (Just between you and me, I would have been horrified at taking a class or reading a book on personal finances. Yuck and double yuck.)

Why then am I writing a book about personal finances?

Simply put, I never want you to go through the pain, shame, and stress that out of control finances can bring to your life.

Sadly, financial struggles are much more common than most people would think.

- **A shocking 70% of Americans today are living paycheck to paycheck.**

- **Financial issues continue to be the number one cause of divorce.**

Most people think financial disaster will never happen to them. I know we sure didn't. Our world was turned upside down when we experienced it.

It wasn't long ago that my family went through a very painful time in our lives where we found ourselves emotionally and financially devastated. It seemed like literally overnight we found ourselves drowning in debt and living a life full of fear, embarrassment and shame. We spent many hours stressing about money and had many sleepless nights.

Fast forward to today, and our family now lives with peace, joy, happiness, and financial abundance. We no longer worry about debt collectors calling our home, unexpected bills lurking in our mailbox, or how we are going to pay for our groceries. I am proud to say that even with four kids and putting our family first, in just three years we have:

- **Paid off over $150,000 worth of debt.**
- **Paid off over $30,000 worth of out-of-pocket medical related expenses.**
- **Learned how to live beyond rich using very simple and easy steps that we now do by investing 5 minutes of our time each day.**

JENSPIRATION

Spending 5 minutes a day on a budget will lead to more riches than spending 2 hours a day in front of the TV.

Think you can't learn how to get a handle on your finances?

Well you can. If a person like me who HATED the word budget and who MAYBE checked their bank accounts once a year can learn how to get a handle on their finances, YOU can too.

This blunt, to the point, no nonsense book will show you how to get your finances under control and get you on the path to living with financial empowerment, peace and joy. The best part is, you only have to spend 5 minutes a day working on your finances with the simple and easy incremental steps I will lay out for you.

Really, 5 minutes is all I need to learning how to live beyond rich?

Yep, if you spend 5 minutes a day paying attention and taking action to gain control of your finances, you will accomplish much more than hours of worrying each day.

Are you tired of worrying about finances?

Well then....let's get going!

Know this before we start...I am delighted that you're starting down your own path to learning how to live beyond rich.

Remember, if I can do it, YOU can too!

Live Beyond Rich! Live Beyond Awesome!

~ Jen McDonough, "The Iron Jen"

Motivational Storyteller. Author, & Coach

Amazon Top 100 Author of *Living Beyond Rich* & *Living Beyond Awesome*

Website: http://www.TheIronJen.com

Twitter: @TheIronJen

Dedicated to:

Those who are seeking financial peace, joy and happiness in their lives.

A word of encouragement from someone "who has been in what seems to be a financially hopeless situation"

- *Know that you are not alone...many have walked in your footsteps before you and many will come after you.*

- *Recognize that there is HOPE and that dreams really do come true when you put intentional actions behind them.*

~ Jen

"Don't Quet™" (Don't Quit)

~ Maggie McDonough

To my family, friends, and readers:

Life is not a straight path; rather, it is a curvy journey. When life tries to knock you down, keep moving forward. Don't Quet (Don't Quit).

Don't sweat the small stuff, just keep moving. Don't Quet (Don't Quit).

Remember your goals can always shift as unexpected life events come your way. It is the intentional incremental steps you do each day that will win the race.

Don't Quet *(Don't Quit)!*

~ Jen McDonough "The Iron Jen"

Contents

PART ONE

LIVING BEYOND RICH PLAN

PART 1

LIVING BEYOND RICH PLAN

JEN'S GEMZ

Live With HOPE!

We have always held to the hope, the belief, the conviction that there is a better life, a better world, beyond the horizon.

~ Franklin D. Roosevelt

CHAPTER 1

Financial Stress - YUCK

Myth: I am the only person to have money problems.

Fact: You are not the first or the last to have money problems.

Stat: 70% of Americans live paycheck to paycheck.
~ Dave Ramsey

‹‹‹‹‹‹‹‹‹‹‹‹‹‹‹‹‹‹‹‹‹‹‹‹‹‹‹‹‹‹‹‹‹

Some of you may be skeptical and questioning if this book is for you. Not long ago, I would have snubbed my nose at reading "this type of book."

Why?

Before our financial storm hit our life, I would have described our family as the typical average American family. We didn't consider ourselves "in debt" or even struggling with finances. The way we lived just seemed normal.

In reality, we had been living "close to the edge" for quite some time, but didn't know it. Why did it take my family nearly losing everything to see our overall financial situation?

When you are struggling with finances, it is always easier to see the overall picture from "outside" in versus looking from the inside out. Shocking, many of the 7 out of 10 people who are living paycheck to paycheck have no clue they are literally one step away from financial disaster.

Is This Worth Your Time Reading?

So is this book really for you? Do you need to get your finances in order?

If you are not sure, take a minute to honestly answer these questions below:

JENSPIRATION

Emergencies never come at a good time. Meet them head on by getting your finances in order.

- **Are you using credit cards for everyday needs such as groceries?**
- **Are you dipping further into your line of credit each month?**
- **Are you finding your money running out before the end of the month?**
- **Are you depending on the equity in your house to finance things?**
- **Do financial emergencies come your way often?**
- **Do you think of money (or the lack of money) often?**
- **Do you dread checking your mailbox as there might be overdue bills waiting for you?**

- Do you jump every time the phone rings in fear it may be another bill collector?
- Do you find anxiety entering your life as money becomes "less available?"
- Do you 'guestimate' your finances rather than use a budget each month?

If you answered yes to any of the questions above, this book is for you!

An Honest Evaluation of Your Situation is Golden

While openly and honestly acknowledging your situation can be frightening, it is so worth it in the long run. **Going through some temporary discomfort is much better than having the experience my family had of waking up one day to find ourselves with a negative bank account balance, maxed out credit cards, an underwater mortgage, no available line of credit and a full blown life emergency standing in our path.**

Seriously, how much time have you wasted when it comes to your personal finances?

Think back on how many hours you have spent worrying, how many nights you laid awake, or how many moments of joy that have passed you by because you were stressed out over your financial situation.

Wouldn't it be nice to have a future without wasting your

precious time on these kinds of worries?

The great news is that once you openly acknowledge the fact that you need help you will be able to start to take strides to unloading the toxic feelings that financial stress has brought to your life.

The Question 'Why' Is an Important Motivator for Your Success

I want to touch on another important aspect in this chapter - exploring the 'WHY' factor.

Knowing the reason WHY you are starting something will help motivate you to:

- **Implement change in your life.**

- **Stay focused on your goals well after the novelty has worn off.**

Why is Personal Finances Important?

Personal finance is MUCH more than just numbers on a piece of paper. It affects all areas of our lives and helps shape our emotional well-being. Left unaddressed, financial struggles can fill your life with an aftermath of debris that will resemble a tornado touching down right smack dab in the middle of your life.

Normal Living Can Be Painful

If financial struggles have so many negatives, why then aren't more people doing something about it?

Sadly, it has become a societal norm. Seriously, think about how common the words bankruptcy, foreclosure, short sale, and chapter 13 are today. Think back 20 years ago - these words weren't so common!

While I go into greater detail on this subject in our book *Living Beyond Rich*, here are a few things to ponder to serve as a wakeup call for many people today.

Disclaimer: Be warned though, some things below may make you mad as they will hit very close to home for some. Know that if any of the statements below do make you mad, I am okay with that. The intent of this book is not to paint a flowery picture, but instead to get you quickly moving towards your freedom journey. Painful facts may not feel very flattering; however, they have been known to act

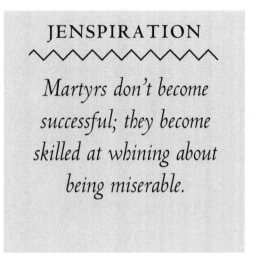

JENSPIRATION

Martyrs don't become successful; they become skilled at whining about being miserable.

as a turning point for many positive life transformations.

Helpful Suggestions to Get You on the Path to Living Beyond Rich Quicker:

1) **Get Out of the Martyr Zone** - Your attitude will play a huge part in how fast you will get your life back in control. Putting yourself into what I call the "Martyr Zone" is another reason to make excuses to stay in your situation, rather than giving yourself permission to seek out solutions. It is all too easy to get into the "poor me" blaming type modes when you are in the middle of a financial mess. Intentionally remind yourself to seek out solutions versus blaming others (I use my Motivational Wristband as a physical reminder to STOP me from going into the Martyr Zone and to remind me to stay on track during times of weakness)

2) **Ditch the Loser Language** - Phrases such as "if only" are prime examples of what I call "loser language that will keep you stuck in the muck":

- If only this wouldn't have happened to ME, I would be okay.
- If only I had more money, I wouldn't have this problem.
- If only my lottery numbers were drawn, I would have it made.

Using the above types of phrases takes the power of personal accountability out of the mix. I want you to use the power of personal accountability to work in your favor. Start intentionally using statements such as:

- **I did**
- **I will**
- **I can**
- **I am**

3) **STOP Using Loser Excuses** - Loser excuses will keep you stuck in the muck. Some prime examples of loser excuses include:

JENSPIRATION

The practice of living on a budget will reduce financial emergencies over time.

- Only those who hold financial degrees can be good at finances. (There are many who are holding financial degrees that are up to their eyeballs in personal debt.)
- I wasn't born with being "good" at finances. (NO ONE was ever "born" being good with finances.)

- Bad things always happen to ME. (Quit whining, they happen to everyone.)

One of the all time biggest user loser excuses is:

JENSPIRATION

∿∿∿∿∿∿

While reality isn't easy to face at times, seeing the overall picture is essential to mapping a journey to success.

"I don't have enough TIME to learn about personal finances."

Why is it the worst excuse?

Too often in our daily lives we put out one fire and move on to the next. **Our days are filled with BUSYNESS — and then we still need to find time to fit in day to day activities with our family and friends.**

Our calendars are filled with endless activities and deadlines. At work, it often feels like our workloads are to the breaking point. Our home life is not much better as we find ourselves running here and there many nights to sporting activities, school activities, religious activities, or other commitments. Without realizing it, we are no longer living our life intentionally…instead we are letting our activities overrun our life. **Pretty soon whenever someone asks how you are doing, the response is "oh, I am BUSY."**

With all this BUSYNESS in your life, you think who has time for learning finances?

If this is one of your excuses, let me toss the question back to you in another way. Who has time for financial stress in their lives? Think about it, financial stress comes with some pretty heavy price tags including:

- **Less work productivity**

- **Burnout**

- **Divorce**

- **Broken relationships**

- **High blood pressure**

- **Strokes**

- **Heart attacks**

- **Shorter life spans**

- **Unhappy lives**

Even the excuse of not having enough time can lead to stress. You stress because you don't have enough time and then you don't make time to address the issue that is causing the stress. It is like a hamster in a wheel going round and round.

You may be questioning the reason for my harshness and wonder "who am I" to make such critical statements.

The simple answer is I was "that person" who used to be in the Martyr zone over our situation. I have used the loser language examples provided and I have used my fair share of loser excuses over the years.

I tell you this honestly, all these types of examples, while it feels "right" or even good at the time, will never propel you forward to create the life you desire.

In addition, the stress of your financial woes can affect other people in your life. As a parent, it affects your kids. As a spouse, it affects your marriage. As an employee, it affects your performance.

I have hammered the above points enough for now. I would encourage you to check out our book *Living Beyond Rich*. It will give you hope, encouragement, and additional tools to get you moving.

For now, let's just look at the simple and easy ways for you to get started on the journey towards a life of freedom. Taking action on your plan will help reduce your stress and through the financial turmoil you may find yourself in.

What will be your first steps?

First, acknowledge the fact that your time is best spent acknowledging your situation, addressing the problem, and seeking out solutions versus choosing to stay in trauma and drama mode.

Second, take a step back for a minute and think how your life might be different today if you didn't need to worry about finances? Can you picture that life? Do you want that life? If so, wouldn't 5 minutes a day be worth it to gain control in your life?

Third, I want you to realize that you CAN take control over your finances, that there is hope, and most importantly, that you are NOT alone. 7 out of 10 people today are living one step away from financial disaster. I want you to be one of the 3 out of 10 people today that are NOT living paycheck to paycheck.

Fourth, realize that while starting your journey to living beyond rich will take some work, it will be totally worth it. Besides, once you get your plan in place, it will literally only take you 5 minutes a day to be intentional on gaining control in your life.

Remember, if I can do it, YOU can too!

∿∿∿∿∿∿∿∿∿∿∿∿∿∿∿∿∿∿∿∿

QUESTIONS TO PONDER:

Have you ever had those blaming type moments in your life?

Do you ever wonder why there seems to be more bills in your mailbox than money in your bank account?

Do you constantly vent about always being broke?

5 MINUTE TIMEOUT

Your personal schedule includes:

- 168 hours per week.

- 24 hours in a day.

- 1440 minutes each day.

If you spent 5 minutes a day on your finances, that would still leave you with:

- 167:25 hours per week.

- 23:55 hours in a day.

- 1435 minutes each day.

JEN'S GEMZ

Live With Conviction —

BELIEVE!

We are what we believe we are.

~ C.S. Lewis

CHAPTER 2

Your Living Beyond Rich Plan

Myth: By sending my kids off to college with a credit card, it teaches them to be responsible with money.

Fact: Lenders are more than willing to teach our kids how to accumulate debt.

Stat: Only 32% of 18-year-olds understand how credit card interest and fees work.

~ Charles Schwab's 2011 Teens & Money Survey

This is the chapter where your plan starts. Are you excited or are you dreading it? Either way is perfectly understandable.

If you are anxious about starting, read this final bit of advice before we start look at your plan.

There are many people out there willing to tell you what to do with your money. **It is easy for most people to get so bogged down in the details of personal finance that they give up on trying to learn it. If this is you, I don't blame you...people can make finances sound extremely complicated.** While there are others who might give you fancy advice that will overwhelm you, I am going to give you the most important basic steps that you can easily implement today.

Admittedly, while there are many important aspects to personal finance, my goal and wish for you is simply this:

- **To have you START and implement your customized Living Beyond Rich plan in the EASIEST and SIMPLEST steps possible.**

So for the over analyzers out there, quit searching for the perfect complicated plan...let's just get you going on A PLAN TODAY.

Here is an overview of what your Living Beyond Rich plan will look like:

1. **Build up $1,000 in a mini emergency fund.**
2. **Pay off all non-mortgage debt.**
3. **Set aside a fully funded emergency fund of 3-6 months worth of expenses.**

That is it. This is what is going to get you out of debt and back in control of your life.

Why are we not touching on the other aspects of finances in this book?

Remember the goal was to:

- **Have you START and implement your customized plan in the EASIEST and SIMPLEST steps possible.**

Too many people get overwhelmed in taking on too much and this is why they fail. You will have plenty of time to

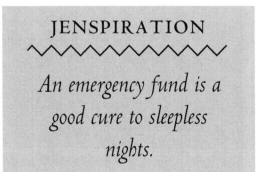

JENSPIRATION

An emergency fund is a good cure to sleepless nights.

check into the other steps to financial wellness after you have gotten your finances under control.

Having said that, I would HIGHLY recommend that you check into our website resources page (http://www.theironjen.com/resources/) for additional in-depth financial programs AFTER you are comfortable with the above three steps and are ready to learn more. The program my family used and wholeheartedly endorses is Dave Ramsey's Financial Peace University program which is listed on our resource page. The steps above are the first three he recommends and the ones that we are going to focus on today.

Ready to get started on creating your customized plan? Okay, then…let's go!

∿∿∿∿∿∿∿∿∿∿∿∿∿∿∿∿∿∿∿∿∿∿

QUESTIONS TO PONDER:

How will I remind myself to keep it EASY and SIMPLE when I start to over think my plan?

Where can I post my plan so I can see it daily?

∿∿∿∿∿∿∿∿∿∿∿∿∿∿∿∿∿∿∿∿∿∿

5 MINUTE TIMEOUT

Average time in front of the TV is 153 hours a month…that is 9,180 precious minutes.

If the average person were to spend 5 minutes a day on their finances, it still leave them with 9,030 minutes of TV watching each month.

JEN'S GEMZ

Live With INTENTION!

Our intention creates our reality.

~ Wayne Dyer

CHAPTER 3

Plan Action Steps Overview

Myth: Everyone should instinctively know how to handle their finances.

Fact: Financial competency is a learned skill.

Stat: Only 43% of 18-year-olds know how to balance a checkbook or check the accuracy of a bank statement. ~ Charles Schwab's 2011 Teens & Money Survey

Here are your simple yet powerful action steps to putting together your Living Beyond Rich Plan (aka your budget):

Step 1: Evaluate - This is where you will review how much:
- ✓ Debt is owed.
- ✓ Income is coming in.
- ✓ Expenses are going out.

Step 2: Plan -This is where you will build the skeleton to your plan by:
- ✓ Writing out your expense categories.
- ✓ Assigning a planned amount to each category.

Step 3: Intentional Action - This is where you will build the muscle by using my TRACC plan:

- ✓ **TRACKING your daily expenses.**
- ✓ **REVIEWING your daily expenses with your planned amounts in each category.**
- ✓ **ADJUSTING as needed.**
- ✓ **CREATING your plan each month.**
- ✓ **COMMITTING to 5 minutes a day.**

If you practice these steps — and incorporate them into your family culture — you will be amazed at the things you will accomplish.

JENSPIRATION

Facing your total debt numbers are crucial to finding peace and resolve. Whatever the number is, at the end of the day it is just a number. It isn't a grade on who you are as a person. . .it is a number.

~~~~~~

QUESTIONS TO PONDER:

What kind of financial emergencies have you had in your own life?

Were you expecting them? How did you deal with them?

Would having an emergency fund help you to rest easier at night?

~~~~~~

5 MINUTE TIMEOUT

If an employee who is experiencing financial stress wastes up to 240 hours per year dealing with personal money matters on the job, wouldn't it be worth teaching them how 5 minutes day can change their lives?

Just imagine what an employee who spends 5 minutes a day on their finances can do to a company's bottom line.

JEN'S GEMZ

Live With COURAGE!

All our dreams can come true, if we have the courage to pursue them.

~ *Walt Disney*

CHAPTER 4

Plan Incremental Steps

Step 1: Evaluate

Myth: Debt is no big deal.

Fact: Debt has become an epidemic.

Stat: U.S. household 2009 debt, including mortgages was at $13.5 trillion. If we divide that among every man, woman and child in America, the average debt is $43,874 per person.
~ The Federal Reserve, March 2010

Let's break your plan down into incremental steps.

Step 1: Evaluate: This will involve reviewing how much:

- Debt is owed.
- Income is coming in.
- Expenses are going out.

First Thing Is Discovering How Much Debt Is Owed
   Speaking from personal experience, this can be the hardest emotional step that you will go through in this process.

This is where you will take an honest look at how much outstanding debt you really have.

Why can this step be so difficult?

Bluntly, many people have no clue how much outstanding debt they have.

Why is this?

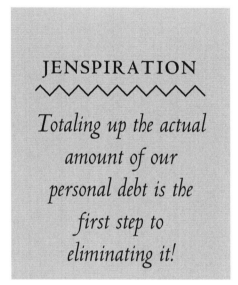

JENSPIRATION

Totaling up the actual amount of our personal debt is the first step to eliminating it!

Partly because we as a society have come to accept that being in debt is just the normal way of living. In addition, savvy marketing has made being in debt seem pretty cool (you can read more about this in our book *Living Beyond Rich*).

Know that even though facing your total amount of debt can be painful, it is so worth it. It will be your first step towards living an abundant life.

Are you ready to get started? Okay, here we go (take a deep breath).

Step A: List out ALL your debts. IMPORTANT: When I say all debts, I mean ALL debts with the exception of your mortgage. Some examples include:

- **Credit cards**

- **Department charge cards**

- **Payday loans**

- **Car loans**
- **College loans**
- **401k loans**
- **Individual loans (i.e relatives, friends)**
- **Medical debt**

Step B: List out beside each debt the interest rate, the date due each month, the total amount owed, and the minimum monthly payment.

Step C: Next list your debts out from smallest amount owed to largest. Sample sheet can look like this:

Debt	% Rate	Due	Total	Minimum
Car #2	9%	1st	$12,145	$475
Visa	29%	15th	$20,753	$150
Car #1	2%	30th	$27,576	$425
Mastercard	15%	21st	$41,275	$325

Step D: Add these up to find out your total debt.

Step E: BREATHE!

That is it. You did it! You took a HUGE step in surpassing most people in our society today by listing out your debts.

How Much Income Is Coming In

Next in your evaluation, list out how much income you have coming in each month

How Much Expenses Are Going Out

Lastly, look at the TOTAL amount of expenses going out each month. Take a minute and compare this number to your monthly income. Are you shocked? If so, know it is very common today to be spending way more than you are earning.

〜〜〜〜〜〜〜〜〜〜〜〜〜〜〜

QUESTIONS TO PONDER:

How do you feel right now looking at your outstanding debt?

How will you use this experience to motivate you through your journey?

〜〜〜〜〜〜〜〜〜〜〜〜〜〜〜

5 MINUTE TIMEOUT

If the average person spends almost 90 minutes each day eating and drinking, wouldn't it be worth putting the fork down for 5 of these minutes?

Imagine what our communities would be like if we were able to feast on the fruits of our future financial wealth instead.

JEN'S GEMZ

Live With FAITH!

Take the first step in faith. You don't have to see the whole staircase, just take the first step.

~ *Martin Luther King, Jr.*

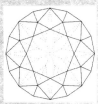

CHAPTER 5

Living Beyond Rich Incremental Steps

Step 2: Plan

Myth: Bankruptcy is an easy way out of a financial crisis.

Fact: Bankruptcy is rated as one of the most stressful life events a person can go through.

Stat: 19% of bankruptcy filers are college students. ~ USA Today

〜〜〜〜〜〜〜〜〜〜〜〜〜〜〜〜〜〜〜

Step 2: Plan: This is where we start building the skeleton to your plan:

1) **Write Out Your Expense Categories** – Visit our sample budget form on our website or visit the Living Beyond Rich Template chapter for a starting point. Do your best to capture expense categories that you regularly spend on. For your debt category, use your

minimum payments. Include the "seasonal" type expenses that come your way such as gifts, insurance, routine car maintenance, school expenses, etc. Go through some of your old bank statements if you need help. Remember you can always adjust these categories as you go.

2) **Assigned a Planned Amount to Each Category -** This is where you start assigning numbers to each category. **If you need to, go back and review past expenses, but remember to set a time limit.** Why a time limit? This step can be a time and energy drainer especially if you are an analyzer type person, a perfectionist, or not a "numbers" type of person. **I would rather have you moving forward on implementing your budget versus becoming stuck on trying to make it perfect. My best advice would be to give it your best shot by setting a manageable time limit on gathering this info and then guessing as best as you can for the rest for the first month or two.** Besides, by month three you should have a pretty good grasp on assigning amounts to each category.

Here are the two main keys to keep in mind for putting together your plan:
- Assign EVERY dollar a name for each month. Meaning EVERY dollar has a purpose - there will be no 'miscellaneous' money anywhere in your budget.
- The GOAL each month is to have a ZERO balance. See the next step on where extra monies are assigned.

3) **How to Assign Any Extra Monies** - This is the fun part of your plan...getting to watch your freedom come to you one dollar at a time.

   In your plan, you have listed off the minimum amounts assigned to pay to each debt. Your goal is to find ways to either bring additional dollars in and/or find ways to cut back. When you have accomplished this, here is your plan for ANY extra income you take in each month (note, if you have a variable income, please see Chapter 14 for one extra added step):

   A. **Mini Emergency Fund $1,000:** Toss any extra money at your mini emergency fund until you have $1,000 saved up. This emergency fund will act as a cushion between you and life. Believe me, you need it so don't go spending it on something you want or THINK you need. This money is ONLY for emergencies.

   B. **Pay Off All Non Mortgage Debt:** After you have your $1,000 mini emergency fund saved up, any extra monies will be tossed at the littlest debt until it is GONE. **This is where you want to attack your debt with EVERY extra dollar you have coming in.** When you have your smallest debt paid off, move the last debt's minimum payment up to the next debt and throw any extra monies at it. Keep ATTACKING your smallest debt until all of your non mortgage debt is eliminated.

   C. **Fully 3-6 Month Fund:** After you have paid off your non mortgage debt, toss any extra monies to fully fund your 3-6 month emergency fund.

QUESTIONS TO PONDER:

Are you ready to start your finance freedom journey or are you allowing excuses to get in your way?

What actions will you take **TODAY** to reach your financial goals?

5 MINUTE TIMEOUT

If the average person sleeps a little over 8 1/2 hours each day, wouldn't it be worth 5 minutes less sleep for worry free slumbers?

JEN'S GEMZ

Live With PASSION!

Every great dream begins with a dreamer. Always remember, you have within you the strength, the patience, and the passion to reach for the stars to change the world.

~ *Harriet Tubman*

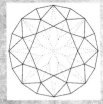

CHAPTER 6

Living Beyond Rich Incremental Steps

Step 3: Intentional Action

Myth: A budget is for people who only have a college degree in finance.

Fact: A budget is for the everyday person who wants to tell their money what to do versus having their money dictate their lives.

Stat: 56% of Americans do not have a budget.

~ 2010 Consumer Financial Literacy Survey

〰〰〰〰〰〰〰〰〰〰〰〰〰〰〰〰〰〰

Step 3: Intentional Action: Now you are ready to start building the muscle around your plan. This is where my TRACC system will help you to start and CONTINUE on your plan:

- **TRACK Your Daily Expenses** - This is when you will start to USE your plan. Start tracking EVERY expense and then log it into your plan.

- **REVIEW Your Daily Expenses With Your Planned Amounts In Each Category** - You want to be able to review and compare what you actually spent versus what you have planned out on a daily basis. You can have the most beautiful looking spreadsheet in the world, but if you don't track your expenses against your plan is worthless.

- **ADJUST as Needed** – As you find categories going over in one area, be sure to adjust as you need to. Your goal is to ensure you have a zero balance each month. You want EVERY dollar to have a name and to be used in an assigned category. If you go over in one category, you are going to need to find another area to take from or find ways to bring in extra income. Remember, EACH dollar has a purpose.

- **CREATE Your Plan Each Month** – NO month is ever going to be perfect and each month will be different. You can always use your plan from the month before to work off of, but realize each month will bring its own challenges and therefore will need to be adjusted accordingly.

- **COMMIT To 5 Minutes a Day** - This is where you will commit 5 minutes a day. Tracking, comparing, and adjusting as you need to.

Why do I suggest you commit to doing this for 5 minutes each day?

One of the biggest reasons I see people fail is that they become overwhelmed with details, they become frustrated, and then they quit or don't even bother starting. Seeing it in 5 minute a day segments is much easier than saying, "Hey, we are going to do a 5 hour

budget session that is going to leave you exhausted, frustrated, and mighty crabby each month." Yuck to that idea!

By breaking the process into an incremental approach, it becomes simple, easy, doable and manageable for just about anyone.

So do yourself a favor and commit to the 5 minute a day approach in tracking, comparing, and adjusting as you need to.

JENSPIRATION

Facing your total debt numbers is crucial to finding peace and resolve. Whatever the number is, at the end of the day it is just a number. It isn't a grade on who you are as a person...it is a number. Remind yourself to look at it in this way and soon you might be sleeping better at night.

QUESTIONS TO PONDER:

Where in your schedule will you commit to

investing 5 minutes a day for your plan?

What systems will you put in place to ensure you will stay on track?

~~~~~~

5 MINUTE TIMEOUT

If on average the typical spends 30-60 minutes each day on food preparation and clean up, wouldn't it be worth taking 5 minutes to healthy finances?

JEN'S GEMZ

Live With MOTIVATION!

If you want to conquer fear, don't sit home and think about it. Go out and get busy.

~ Dale Carnegie

CHAPTER 7

Living Beyond Rich Overview

Myth: My spouse and I can't get along when it comes to money.

Fact: Couples from all backgrounds have learned to get on the same page when it comes to money.

Stat: Money issues are the number one cause of divorce. ~ Dave Ramsey

Living Beyond Rich Plan Overview:

1. Build up your $1,000 mini emergency fund.
2. Pay off all your non mortgage debt.
3. Set aside your fully funded emergency fund of 3-6 months of expenses.

Action Steps for Your Living Beyond Rich Plan Overview:

- **Step 1: Evaluate -** This is where you will review how much:
    - ✓ Debt is owed.
    - ✓ Income is coming in.

✓ Expenses are going out.

- **Step 2: Plan** -This is where you will build the skeleton to your plan by:
    ✓ Writing out your expense categories.
    ✓ Assigning a planned amount to each category.

- **Step 3: Intentional Action** – This is where you will build the muscle around your plan using my TRACC system:
    o **TRACK** your daily expenses.
    o **REVIEW** your daily expenses with your planned amounts in each category.
    o **ADJUST** as needed.
    o **CREATE** your plan each month.
    o **COMMIT** to 5 minutes a day.

〰〰〰〰〰〰〰〰〰〰〰〰〰〰〰〰〰

QUESTIONS TO PONDER:

How will your life play out by spending 5 minutes a day on your finances?

Are you using goals and solutions to transform your financial life into the life you desire?

〰〰〰〰〰〰〰〰〰〰〰〰〰〰〰〰〰

5 MINUTE TIMEOUT

According to the 2011 Bureau of Labor Statistics, we spend an average of 30-60 minutes each day doing housework.

Imagine what our finances would look like if we spent only 5 minutes cleaning up our finances instead.

JEN'S GEMZ

Live With PERSEVERANCE!

A hero is an ordinary individual who finds the strength to persevere and endure in spite of overwhelming obstacles.

~ Christopher Reeve

CHAPTER 8

Final Words of Wisdom

Myth: The little guy can't get ahead.

Fact: According to Tom Stanley's book, *The Millionaire Next Door*, the majority of millionaires today are made up of ordinary everyday people and NOT the rich and famous as most assume.

Stat: 28% of Americans admit to not paying all their bills on time. ~ 2010 Consumer Financial Literacy Survey

Some important things to keep in mind while you go through this process...

Causes of Debt

An important step to gaining control in your finances is recognizing that financial struggles can basically be boiled down to one or both of these causes:

1. **Lack of income and/or**
2. **Overspending**

Oh, I can tell some of you may have gotten mad at this statement and I get it. It was very hard to accept this basic truth when we first started. I remember wanting to yell, "HEY, it is NOT my fault my car broke down, it is not my fault that medical conditions struck our family, it is not my fault my company closed its doors, etc."

The truth is whether or not outside factors played a part in how you arrived at your current situation, the facts are still the facts. You are in your situation today most likely because of lack of income to meet your current expenses and/or you have overspending issues.

An example of this is being overweight. According to the National Heart Lung and Blood Institute, ***"Overweight and obesity happen over time when you take in more calories than you use."***

In other words, being overweight is caused by excess of food and/or a lack of exercise.

You may say, "yes, but my situation is different because of _____(you fill in the blank).

Yes, it is true, there are sometimes outside factors that affect our situations, HOWEVER, the fact still remains that weight issues are primarily caused by the ratio of calories in versus calories burned…the same is true for finances.

- **Finance issues are directly related to either lack of income and/or overspending issues EVEN when outside factors play a part in your situation.**

By identifying the cause(s), it may help you to put boundaries around the source of financial stress and serve as an aid to help you focus on finding solutions.

Earning Extra Income

If lack of income is the main cause of your financial distress, go out there and figure out a way to earn more income. For a more detailed explanation on how our family managed to have 10 W-2 forms in 2010, pick up a copy of our book *Living Beyond Rich*. We were able to work so many jobs even with working around our four kids. In addition it was:

- During a downturned economy.
- Involved going through an emotional job loss.
- When we had our fourth child.
- When we were flying back and forth for medical treatments for our son.
- When I had H1N1 during my second trimester.
- When my husband and I both underwent unplanned/unexpected surgeries.

In short, when you start focusing on what you CAN do rather than what you CANNOT do you will start to see opportunities all around you.

My last piece of advice is to look for ways to bring in extra income by finding places or persons that could use your help and then offer to be of service. Don't wait for them to ask you. By becoming BOLD and COURAGEOUS you will be amazed at the opportunities that open up. Some examples include:

- Seek out busy pizza places and offer to become a delivery person.
- Offer to cut grass or shovel snow in nearby housing developments.
- Offer to become a contracted driver for furniture stores.
- Become a weekend or overnight babysitter for those people that work off hours.

- Become a coach or tutor.

STOP depending on places to put up a help wanted sign and go make yourself available. This is when opportunities will start to open up.

Lastly, remember to ASK, ASK, ASK. Connect with people you know to let them know you are looking for ways to earn extra income. The old saying, "it isn't what you know, but who you know" is very true when it comes to job hunting.

For more information on this topic, I highly encourage you check out Dan Miller's book, *No More Dreaded Mondays* or check out his free podcast or website for more information.

Evaluating Wants Versus Needs

I go more into detail in our book *Living Beyond Rich,* but basically the truth is that our society has a twisted view of what our true wants are compared to our true needs. Things such as cable TV, going out to eat, sporting activities, expensive vacations, etc. are expectations for many people today when in reality, these types of things are really extras we can do without.

If you are able to afford your "wants" in your plan and it is worth it to you, then great, add them in. Personally, the process of realizing what our needs are over our wants has been freeing. By doing this, we were able to choose to cut back on our wants in order to pay off our debt sooner. This allowed us to live the life we wanted much faster. So do you need to cut out all your fun? Absolutely not, however, if you are coming up with a negative balance each month, I highly suggest you take a look at where your money is going and cut out some of those wants.

Seeking Out Solutions

Once you have identified opportunities for

improvement, continue your evaluation by thinking constructively. Financial stress is lessened when you are empowered to take control of your situation. This is done by continuously seeking out solutions versus wasting your time on blaming.

Remembering that you were not born knowing how to handle finances will help you be more open to learning about finances.

Words of Advice

- **Goals:** Set some long term and short term goals for yourself. Where do you want to be in 1 month, 1 year, 2 years, 5 years, etc. (visit our resource site for our FREE SMARTIE Goals worksheet).

- **Celebrate:** Remember to acknowledge and celebrate the victories in both your short and long term goals. Examples of short term celebrations could include:
  - ✓ Celebrating the first month of successfully living on your finance plan.
  - ✓ Celebrating paying off your first debt.
  - ✓ Celebrating your first successful trip to the store without any impulse purchases.

- **Sticking to Your Goals**: If you find yourself having a hard time setting up your goals and sticking to them, put systems in place to help you stay on task. Ideas include:
  - ✓ Join or better yet start a mentor group.
  - ✓ Meet with a coach, mentor, or counselor.
  - ✓ Seek out employee assistance options through your employer.
  - ✓ Enlist help from your local church.

✓ Participate in a financial program or workshop.
✓ Listen to podcasts and/or read blogs.

- **Emotional Issues**: If you are dealing with emotional issues such as a death of a loved one, divorce, medical issues, job loss, etc. don't be afraid to ask for help from others. Having the help of others who are not emotionally involved can mean a world of difference in helping you through painful times. See the list above for some ideas. Know we all need help at times in our lives.

- **Journal**: Take time out to journal. It will help you see your situation in a clearer sense and will be rewarding to look back on how far you have come.

- **Build Your Trusted Team Members**: Consider enlisting the support of others that will encourage you along the way such as coaches, TRUSTED friends, mentors, counselors, podcasts, blogs, forums, etc. Word of caution: STAY AWAY FROM THE NEGATIVE NELLIES of the world as there are plenty of them out there. Know that not everyone is going to be excited for your new success in life. Accept this as a fact and don't be disappointed when you find some of these people in your life. You only have so much energy during the day, don't waste it on someone who is going to steal your joy. **Look for those people who are going to build you up and encourage you on the way.**

- **Attitude in Facing Outside Factors:** In some cases, you will not be able to eliminate the source of outside stress factors overnight. This is especially true if you are dealing with a job loss, medical issues, dealing with past due debt collectors, foreclosures, etc. Keep in mind this one piece of advice. **As long as you are taking ACTION to getting your finances in order, you need to let go of the things you can't control.** By giving yourself permission to release any feelings of guilt, fear, worry, and panic, you will have more energy to focus on solutions.

- **Examples of Actions for Outside Factors:** Actions you can take when outside factors are adding financial stress to your life can include:

JENSPIRATION

Financing $5 on a credit card each day for coffee is stealing $1,865 a year from one's freedom when you are in debt.

  - ✓ If you think you may be in jeopardy of losing your job, take action to start looking for a new job today (See our resources page for Dan Miller's 48days.com site).
  - ✓ If you know you are going to have large amounts of medical bills, take action to work out management payment plans with your providers (See bonus chapter on Medical Debt).

- **Plan Name** – Whether you decide to call it your budget, your Financial Freedom Plan, your Living

Beyond Rich plan, etc. know that it is a plan where you are telling your money WHAT to do versus having your money tell YOU what to do. Your plan is not meant to be thought of as a straightjacket; rather it represents your future freedom. Become empowered and name it what you want.

- **Ditch Your Credit Cards**: Do yourself an enormous favor and STOP using credit cards. I go into this more in my *Living Beyond Rich* book, but basically studies have shown that you will spend 40% more when using a credit card versus cash. Bottom line, don't try to outsmart the credit card companies – just skip using them altogether.

- **Get Mad at Debt** – That's right, get MAD at your debt. Get rid of it and never let it come back.

Bonus Tips for Married Couples:

- Before you start, realize that getting on the same page with finances and learning how to live with intention each day takes time and practice.

- **Involve your spouse in the process if they are willing and talk openly about it WITHOUT BLAMING.** Financial stress has enough guilt associated with it; you don't need to add to it by having a crappy or crabby attitude when going through this process. Look at it as gathering info that will lead you towards financial freedom. The past is past; you can't do anything about it. Be excited that you are driving your family towards a better future. Remember that money issues are the number one cause of divorce and by taking charge of your situation you are helping your marriage and your quality of life. **Be encouraging and supportive whenever possible.**

- Seriously don't argue over the little stuff. If you "lose" a few battles, but in the end it lets you "win the war", then loosen up and remember to keep the big picture in mind.

- To help you and your spouse come up with a workable plan, consider each other's goals, priorities, personalities, and learning styles. Solutions that may work for one person may not work for another. **In addition, be sure you both are involved in seeking out the root of the problem (again WITHOUT BLAMING).** For example, ask yourself how you can change your own attitude rather than trying to change your spouse.

When we first started, I wanted to take EVERYTHING fun out of life for the next 10 years. Adding to it, I talked about the plan ALL the time and in the process, turned my spouse off to getting on board. I would get so irritated when I found a charge that he didn't account for.

JENSPIRATION

Imperfection is a part of life...embrace it, learn from it, and triumph.

Patience, encouragement, and persistence were the three keys in getting my own spouse on board.

Once he was able to start seeing results and understand that we were really working towards having a better future he was able to join in. (Visit our resources page for Reluctant Spouse article http://www.theironjen.com/worksheets/ .)

Final Points

- **YOU Are In Control of YOUR Actions** - Financial stress seldom if ever goes away by itself. It can worsen until one day your health, career, family, or life balance is affected. Take these painful situations as a reason to start evaluating your financial situation and finding solutions in order to create the life you want to live. Remember, you cannot control everything but YOU CAN take control of your own attitudes and actions.

- **YOU Can Learn This Stuff** - Personal finance is a learnable skill and not something you were born knowing. Investing some time in learning a little about it and following a budget may cause you to cut back on some things in your life such as watching TV (note, the average person today watches 153 hours of TV per month according to the 2009 Nielsen reports), but it will be well worth it in the end.

- **YOU Can Become Successful** –You will get to your end goal faster by staying intentionally focused and

62

motivated. Know this though - whether you get there quickly or not, the important thing to keep in mind is that you are taking intentional action to get to your goal.

- **YOU Are Awesome** - Give yourself credit for reading this book. If you are embarrassed or ashamed, remember the past is the past so let it go. You now are taking ACTION to gain control of your future. For that, I say I am proud of you!

- **Suggestions on Next Steps** – AFTER you have become comfortable with the process of setting up and using your plan, I would highly encourage you to set aside time to continue learning about personal finances. How? Connect with me through one of our workshops, read our book *Living Beyond Rich*, check out our free resources through my website, have me speak at your upcoming event, or connect with me on through my coaching sessions.

Lastly, when you want change in your life, remember to MOVE IT and don't quet (don't quit).

Remember, if I can do it, YOU can do it!

~~~~~~~~~~~~~~~~~~~~~~~~~~~~~~~~~~~

FINAL QUESTIONS FROM JEN TO PONDER:

Do you have empowerment, peace, and joy over your finances?

If not, are you ready to become intentional and choose your pivotal date of transformation?

Where will you be tomorrow? In the next 5 years? In the next 10 years? In the next 20 years?

If you don't start today, what makes you think tomorrow will be any different?

Are you ready to starting Living Beyond Rich? If so my friends, I will look forward to seeing you at the top!

~~~~~~~~~~~~~~~~~~~~~~~~~~~~~~~~~~~

5 MINUTE TIMEOUT

Imagine yourself spending 300 seconds a day on your finances. Wouldn't it be worth ditching the stress, embarrassment, worry, or shame for the low cost of 5 minutes a day?

If I can do it, **YOU CAN** do it.

PART II
Bonus
Section

JEN'S GEMZ

Live With PURPOSE!

Success demands singleness of purpose.
~ *Vince Lombardi*

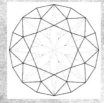

CHAPTER 9

LIVING BEYOND RICH CONTRACT

If you want to change your financial situation, I encourage you to start by saying out loud:

"I believe in myself! Today is my day! Today I start my freedom finance journey!"

Why not take it a step further and write it down?

"I will commit to investing in myself in order to live an awesome life filled with empowerment and peace. By believing in myself, I know I will succeed on my freedom finance journey in order to

Live a Life of Awesomeness™."

An awesome financial life to me would look like:

_____
_____
_____
_____
_____
_____
_____
_____
_____
_____

When I look back, I want to remember why I started my freedom finance journey. I started because:

_____
_____
_____
_____
_____
_____
_____
_____
_____
_____

My goals for the next month include:

1.

2.

3.

My goals for the year include:

1.

2.

3.

My goals for next 5 years include:

1.

2.

3.

When I hit low points in my journey, resources I will turn to as a source of encouragement include:

1.

2.

3.

The mentors, accountability partners, friends, etc. I commit to intentionally meet with on a regular basis to help me on my journey include:

1.

2.

3.

My name is: _____

and on this date: _____

I took my first steps to gaining freedom, peace, and empowerment in my life.

Congratulations on taking your first steps to Living Beyond Rich™!

CHAPTER 10

∿∿∿∿∿∿∿∿∿∿∿∿

Reluctant Spouse Tips

Help! I Have a Reluctant Spouse

How the heck does one get their reluctant spouse on board with this finance stuff?

Being that money issues are the number one cause for divorce today, it is not surprising that having a reluctant spouse is common. This is due to many reasons including:

- What our beliefs are.

- How our parents handled finances.

- The circumstances under which we were raised.

- What our personality types are.

- What experiences we encounter as adults.

Regardless of the reasons why, it is frustrating for both parties when we are sitting on opposite sides of the money fence.

So what are some ways to get a reluctant spouse on board?

First, we need to understand and respect that everyone handles and processes things differently. Once we acknowledge this fact, we can find solutions. Some solutions that may help for your family include:

1. **Learning Style** — Understand how your spouse processes information. Are they a visual, auditory, or a kinesthetic learner? Would your spouse more likely read a book, watch a video, or just wing it and learn as they go?

2. **Personality Style** — What are your personality styles? An extrovert might enjoy financial classes that are offered in groups. An introvert may prefer to either read a book or watch a video online. Investing a few minutes and dollars into personality profiles such as the DISC profile (information can be found on our website) is well worth it.

3. **Outside Influences** — Is your spouse influenced by others around them? Whose opinions do they value? Find those people and tap into them for assistance. Ideas include mentors, friends, counselors, coaches, pastoral staff, colleagues, and relatives.

4. **Communication** — How are you presenting this information to your spouse? Are you nagging or encouraging them about finances? Are they only hearing what is being taken away from them or are you talking about goals and dreams? Are you quoting others as being experts and are they are seeing that as being a threat and/or disrespectful? How can you help improve communication? Some ideas include:

    • **Dreams/Goals** — Talk about the reasons why you want to change your finances. Listen to your spouse's dreams and what they would want to do if your family was financially free. Stop talking about what is only being taken away and focus rather on what lay ahead. The sacrifices you today will hold incredible rewards tomorrow.

- **Include** — Involve your spouse, don't run them over. Remember, it is always easier to walk with someone rather than to push or pull them along.

- **Compromise** — Compromise when needed on the small things in order to get to the big things that are important. For example, if you are disagreeing on the amount on budgeted grocery expenses, as long as your budget isn't going over and you are making progress to your goal, take a chill pill and ease up. If it slows up your progress a bit, that is okay. Much better to arrive at the finish line together versus either not arriving at all or arriving separately.

5. **Trust and Actions** — Are your past actions affecting your spouse's trust level? Do you have a history of not following through on things, rushing into dead end quick rich schemes, etc? If so, what action steps can you take to earn your spouse's trust? Ideas include:

- **Progress** — Set goals together and follow up on them regularly. Where are you at with your short-term goals (i.e. are you tracking your expenses each day, logging expenses, staying within budget, etc.) and your long-term goals (i.e. how much debt has been eliminated, how much to go before that dream vacation or whatever your goals and dreams are, etc.)?

- **Meet Regularly** — Turning off the TV for 30 minutes each week to speak face to face with NO interruptions will help not only your finances, but also help strengthen your marriage.

- **Be Consistent** — Stay focused and remain consistent on your promises and actions. If you struggle in remaining consistent, visit my SMARTIE goal tips.

- **Tools** — Is your family equipped with the appropriate tools, support, and resources? If not, talk about solutions on how to find valuable tools, support, and resources (see our website for ideas).

Lastly, realize that debt may only be the symptom to a much deeper problem such as communication issues. If this is the case, consider seeking out professional guidance for help. Suggestions on where to find help include:

- **Church**

- **EAP (Employee Assistance Program) through employers**

- **Counselors**

- **Trusted advisors**

- **Coaches**

While isn't always easy getting on the same page with your finances, please know it will be so worth it for those that can. Take advantage of the worksheets below to work your way to finding solutions if you find yourself with a reluctant spouse.

Helpful Worksheets:

1. **Learning Style** — Understand how your spouse processes information. Are they a visual, auditory, or a kinesthetic learner? Would your spouse more likely read a book, watch a video, or just wing it and learn as they go?

Q1: What learning style will work for me?

_____
_____
_____
_____
_____
_____
_____

Q2: What learning style will work for my spouse?

_____
_____
_____
_____
_____
_____
_____

Q3: What ways can I take action in finding solutions versus blaming or whining?

_____

_____

_____

_____

_____

_____

_____

2. **Personality Style** — What are your personality styles? An extrovert might enjoy financial classes that are offered in groups. An introvert may prefer to either read a book or watch a video online. Investing a few minutes and dollars into personality profiles such as the DISC profile (information can be found on our website) is well worth it.

Q1: How will my personality style work in learning this?

_____

_____

_____

_____

_____

_____

_____

Q2: How will my spouse's personality style work in learning this?

_____

_____

_____

_____

_____

_____

_____

_____

_____

Q3: What ways can I take action in finding solutions versus blaming or whining?

_____

_____

_____

_____

_____

_____

_____

_____

_____

3. **Outside Influences** — Is your spouse influenced by others around them? Whose opinions do they value? Find those people and tap into them for assistance. Ideas include mentors, friends, counselors, coaches, pastoral staff, colleagues, and relatives.

Q1: What persons influence my life?

_____
_____
_____
_____
_____
_____
_____

Q2: What persons influence my spouse's life?

_____
_____
_____
_____
_____
_____
_____
_____

Q3: What ways can I take action in finding solutions versus blaming or whining?

_____

_____

_____

_____

_____

_____

_____

_____

_____

4. **Communication** — How are you presenting this information to your spouse? Are you nagging or encouraging them about finances? Are they only hearing what is being taken away from them or are you talking about goals and dreams? Are you quoting others as being experts and are they seeing that as being a threat and/or disrespectful? How can you help improve communication? Some ideas include:

✓ **Dreams/Goals** — Talk about the reasons why you want to change your finances. Listen to your spouse's dreams and what they would want to do if your family was financially free. Stop talking about what is only being taken away and focus rather on what lay ahead.

✓ **Include** — Involve your spouse, don't run them over. Remember, it is always easier to walk with someone rather than to push or pull them along.

✓ **Compromise** — Compromise when needed on the small things in order to get to the big things that are important. For example, if you are disagreeing on the amount on budgeted grocery expenses, as long as your budget isn't going over and you are making progress to your goal, take a chill pill and ease up. If it slows up your progress a bit, that is okay. Much better to arrive at the finish line together versus either not arriving at all or arriving separately.

Q1: What way can I be successful in working with my spouse?

_____
_____
_____
_____
_____
_____

Q2: What way can my spouse help me be successful in working with him/her?

_____

_____

_____

_____

_____

_____

_____

_____

Q3: What ways can I take action in finding solutions versus blaming or whining?

_____

_____

_____

_____

_____

_____

_____

_____

_____

5. **Trust and Actions** — Are your past actions affecting your spouse's trust level? Do you have a history of not following through on things, rushing into dead end quick rich schemes, etc? If so, what action steps can you take to earn your spouse's trust? Ideas include:

✓ **Progress** — Set goals together and follow up on them regularly. Where are you at with your short-term goals (i.e. are you tracking your expenses each day, logging expenses, staying within budget, etc.) and your long-term goals (i.e. how much debt has been eliminated, how much to go before that dream vacation or whatever your goals and dreams are, etc.)?

✓ **Meet Regularly** — Turning off the TV for 30 minutes each week to speak face to face with NO interruptions will help not only your finances, but also help strengthen your marriage.

✓ **Be Consistent** — Stay focused and remain consistent on your promises and actions. If you struggle in remaining consistent, revisit my SMARTIE Goal tips.

✓ **Tools** — Is your family equipped with the appropriate tools, support, and resources? If not, talk about solutions on how to find valuable tools, support, and resources (see our website for ideas).

Q1: What action steps can I take to earn my spouse's trust and support?

_____
_____
_____
_____
_____
_____
_____
_____

Q2: What can my spouse do to earn my trust and support?

_____
_____
_____
_____
_____
_____
_____
_____
_____

Q3: What ways can I take action in finding solutions versus blaming or whining?

_____

_____

_____

_____

_____

_____

_____

_____

_____

6. Lastly, realize that debt may only be the symptom to a much deeper problem such as communication issues. If this is the case, consider seeking out professional guidance for help. Suggestions on where to find help include:

> → Church

> → EAP (Employee Assistance Program) through employers

> → Counselors

> → Trusted advisors

> → Coaches

Q1: What will I commit to if my spouse and I are having a difficult time getting on the same page?

_____
_____
_____
_____
_____
_____
_____
_____

Q2: What will your spouse consider in working through this difficult time to get on the same page?

_____
_____
_____
_____
_____
_____
_____
_____

Q3: What ways can I take action in finding solutions versus blaming or whining?

_____
_____
_____
_____
_____
_____

_____

_____

Remember personal accountability will take you farther in becoming successful than blaming.

JEN'S GEMZ

Live With RESILIENCE!

Character cannot be developed in ease and quiet. Only through experience of trial and suffering can the soul be strengthened, ambition inspired, and success achieved.

~ Helen Keller

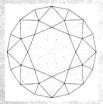

CHAPTER 11

Living Beyond Rich Template

‹‹‹‹‹‹‹‹‹‹‹‹‹‹‹‹‹‹‹‹‹‹‹‹‹‹‹‹‹‹‹‹

Please visit our website for our free downloadable budget worksheet.

Please always remember that if you are unable to make your monthly expenses, the first important items to get in your budget will be:
- ✓ **Basic Housing**
- ✓ **Basic Utilities (this does not include luxury items such as cable TV, internet phone service, etc.)**
- ✓ **Basic Food (no dining out or fast food)**
- ✓ **Basic Transportation (you don't need a $500 a month car to drive)**

No matter what debt collector is calling, remember the above budget items come FIRST.

Here are some recommended budget categories to help you get started:

✓ Charity:
1. Intentional Charity
2. Fun Charity
3. Church

✓ Savings
1. Emergency Savings
2. Set aside Tax Account
3. College Savings

✓ Housing
1. 1st Mortgage / Rent
2. 2nd Mortgage
3. Home Repairs
4. Routine Maintenance

✓ Utilities
1. Gas / Electric / Oil
2. Water / Sewer
3. Trash
4. Home Telephone
5. Internet
6. Cell Phone

✓ Food
1. Groceries
2. Fast Food
3. Dining Out (NOT Fast Food)
4. Child(ren) School Lunches

✓ Transportation
1. Car Replacement Fund
2. Fuel
3. Repair / Maintenance
4. Parking
5. Public Transportation
6. Car / License Registration Fees

✓ Clothing
1. Adult Clothes
2. Child(ren) Clothes
3. Work Clothes

✓ Medical / Health
1. Medical Premiums
2. Clinic / Physician Charges
3. Facility Charges
4. HSA Monthly
5. Prescriptions
6. Life / Disability Insurance

✓ Personal
1. Child Care
2. Child / Spousal Support
3. Gifts
4. School Expenses
5. Hair Care/ Skin Care / Make Up
6. Membership Expenses
7. Print Subscriptions
8. Allowances
9. Child(ren) Sports
10. Adult Sports
11. Personal Growth

✓ Entertainment
1. Books / Music
2. Video / DVD Rentals
3. Movies / Plays
4. Concerts / Clubs
5. Cable TV

✓ Debts
1. Credit Cards
2. Department Store Credit Cards
3. Car Payments
4. Student Loans
5. Personal Loans
6. Miscellaneous debts

JEN'S GEMZ

Live With GRATITUDE!

As we express our gratitude, we must never forget that the highest appreciation is not to utter words, but to live by them.

~ *John F. Kennedy*

CHAPTER 12

Journaling: A Powerful Tool

∿∿∿∿∿∿∿∿∿∿∿∿∿∿∿∿∿∿∿∿∿∿

Journaling can not only be therapeutic, but can help you see where you have been and where you are going.

It is also a great way to celebrate your victories on days when you feel like you are not making progress.

Reference back to your Living Beyond Rich contract – why did you start, what would you like to accomplish in the next month, year, and 5 years. What was life like and how would you like it to be?

Spend 5-10 minutes each week jotting down your thoughts, your feelings, your goals, your struggles, or whatever is weighing on your mind.

Remember, it doesn't have to be perfect…this is simply your thoughts to look back on. Even if you never look back at this journal, it helps will help you through the process of seeking out solutions

My Journal Notes

Date:

My Journal Notes

Date:

My Journal Notes

Date:

My Journal Notes

Date:

JEN'S GEMZ

Live With Action!

People are always blaming their circumstances for what they are. I don't believe in circumstances. The people who get on in this world are the people who get up and look for the circumstances they want, and if they can't find them, make them.

~ George Bernard Shaw

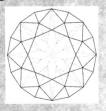

CHAPTER 13

How to Gain More Time

∿∿∿∿∿∿∿∿∿∿∿∿∿∿∿∿∿

How to Become a Time Management Expert

People looking to earn more time and extra income will benefit from using time management skills.

What are the keys to using our allotted 168 hours per week to the fullest?

Planning and intentional living are the answers. Much like our financial budget, our time can be budgeted in the same way.

Successful time management skills can be enhanced by:

- **Identifying goals.**
- **Identifying priorities.**
- **Focusing on solutions instead of excuses.**

Looking at what we can do with our 168 hours versus what we can't do will lead to more opportunities for generating extra income.

In my book *Living Beyond Awesome*, I talk about learning how to become intentional with time and resources while training for an Ironman Triathlon (2.4 mile swim, 112 mile bike ride, and a 26.2 mile run within 17 hours). My priorities were to be a great mom and wife first while maintaining a full-time career and a household. My primary goal was to complete Ironman. Here is an example of what my training week looked like:

- *20 hours training*

- *5 hours of travel, prep time (getting equipment ready, etc.) and wrap up time (showered, dressed, etc.)*

- *40 hours at work*

- *12 hours of commute time*

- *49 hours of sleep (7 hours a night)*

- *10 hours of movies with the family (No TV shows allowed)*

- *2 hours for church*

This left me with about 30 hours if everything went as planned to spend with my family, get our grocery shopping done, do some general house chores, etc. This sounds like a lot of time to spare, but really, it wasn't. It takes serious discipline not to whittle these valuable hours away on useless things that added no value to my priorities and goals. TV was a prime example of what I stayed away from....it's basically one of those mindless (non)activities that only serves to rob us of productive time.

Tips for Gaining Time:

- **Tracking** — Track your time to see where you are spending it. Be honest in your tracking — are there things you can cut out? Are the activities you are filling your time with matching up with your goals and priorities? Give yourself permission to drop the items off that don't fall on your priority list. Focused effort leads to intentional living.

- **Schedule** — List your schedule out. If you need more

time…budget it out much like you do with your money. Don't like your schedule? Be intentional and change it.

- **Task Lists** — List out your daily tasks. You can gain up to two hours worth of productivity each day when you use daily task lists. Where can you keep your list so you will actually use it each day?

- **Priorities** — List your priorities in life out. What comes first, second, and third?

- **Goals** — List your goals out using the SMARTIE method which is available under our website resources. Be sure these goals fit into what your top priorities are.

- **Prioritization** — Life is not linear. Continuously prioritizing our priorities and goals to match our use of time is essential to successful time management.

Remember…it isn't JUST 168 hours per week to waste; you HAVE a gift of 168 hours a week to use wisely.

CHAPTER 14

Help! I have a Variable Income

~~~~~~~~~~~~~~~~~~~~~~~~~~~~~~~~~~~~

What To Do When You Have a Variable Income

For those that have a variable income, know that your Living Beyond Rich plan is very doable. Your plan will be exactly the same except for an extra step added in right after you complete the first step of saving up your $1,000 mini emergency fund.

This step will be setting up and utilizing your Variable Income Account.

First Step: Figuring Out Your Averages
To set up this account, you will need to determine these three things:
1. **Monthly Income** - Discover what your monthly income is. If you are not sure, find out your yearly income and divide it by 12.
2. **Average Number of Months** - Figure out how many months in a row that it takes to determine your average income. For example, you may not have the same amount

of income on a monthly basis, but perhaps you can predict what you can make on a three month average. If you are not sure, take your best guess. Over time you can refine this. For now, we want you started on your plan.

3. **Lowest Monthly Income** – Determine your lowest monthly income.

Second Step: How Much to Put In Your Variable Income Account

Your next step will be to determine how much to put in your Variable Income Account by going through these two steps:

1. **Potential Monthly Shortfall** - Determine the difference between your average income and your lowest income. This is your monthly potential shortfall. For example if your average monthly income is $100 a month and your lowest income is $10, you know you have a potential $90 shortfall each month.

2. **Variable Income Target** - Multiply your potential monthly shortfall by your predictable average months. For example, using the above example if you know your average number of months to gain a consistent average income is 3 months, you would multiply your $90 shortfall by 3 months. This determines the amount you want in your Variable Income Account which in this case would be $270.

Third Step: Using Your Variable Income Account

Finally, you are ready to set up and use your Variable Income Account by doing the following.

1. AFTER you have your mini emergency fund of $1,000 saved up, you will want to start putting your the targeted amount of money away in an account set aside for your Variable Income Account.

2. As you run into your shortfall months, you will pull the difference from the money you are short to the average monthly income from your Variable Income Account.

3. On months you have extra income, replace any monies up to your targeted amount.

4. AFTER you have reached your target Variable Income amount, continue to apply your extra monies to the next step in your plan (i.e. paying off debt or saving up for your fully funded emergency fund).

Note: It is important to remain disciplined in sticking to your plan on the months when you are bringing in extra income. Your Variable Income Account is to bring stability into your life....NOT extra toys.

CHAPTER 15

Goal-Setting Tips

∧∧∧∧∧∧∧∧∧∧∧∧∧∧∧∧∧∧∧∧∧∧∧∧∧∧∧∧∧∧∧∧∧∧

Goals just rock! They are the destination to our finish line. We can set our sights on a goal then aim for it.

What are some awesome goal techniques I have picked up over the years?

My SMARTIE goal method has been incredibly helpful in my many endeavors throughout the years.

Jen's SMARTIE Goal Tips:

S: Specific! Successful goals are specific written goals.

M: Measurable! Goals require measurable outcomes with timelines along with milestones along the way to mark your progress.

A: Action! Goals require action!

R: Reach! Set goals that require you to stretch and reach out of your comfort zone.

T: Track! Track your progress consistently and review your progress regularly.

I: Incremental! Long-term goals that are worth accomplishing will be conquered in incremental steps over time, NOT overnight.

E: Enjoy! Make sure as you hit your milestones that you take time to celebrate and enjoy!

Along with SMARTIE goals, what are some great tips?

- **Write your specific goals down no matter how impossible they seem.**

- **Keep them in a place where you see them each and every day.**

- **Make a list each week of the 2-3 things you want to accomplish each day/week to hit your short-term goals that lead to your long-term goals.**

- **Visualize accomplishing your goals regularly.**

- **Say them out loud.**

- **Share them with your trusted advisors and keep them from the Negative Nellies in your life.**

- **Keep in mind that victory is won with intentional incremental steps toward your goal.**

A great example of one of my real goals I used in completing Ironman included:

- **Complete Ironman Triathlon on November 1st in less than 14 hours.**
  - * **Finish the 2.4 mile swim in less than 2 hours and 20 minutes without drowning.**
    - ◊ **Take 6 Total Immersion swimming lessons to learn how to swim by February 1st.**

Along with my main goal, you can see I broke my swim portion of the event into smaller incremental goals. After each incremental goal was accomplished, I took time to look back and enjoy.

Let goals become your launch pad to success!

CHAPTER 16

Budget Tool Suggestions

∿∿∿∿∿∿∿∿∿∿∿∿∿∿∿∿∿∿∿∿∿∿

Whatever budgeting tool you decide on, pick one that you will USE. Using a budgeting tool is essential to your financial success. Here are some suggestions:

- Notepad

- Excel

- Crown Financial (http://crownfinancial.org) — Plenty of free resources for budgets

- **YNAB (You Need A Budget (http://www.YNAB.com)** — Paid template download that is very popular.

- **My Total MoneyMakeover (http://mytotalmoneymakeover.com)** — Dave Ramsey's paid subscription program (this is what we used during our journey).

CHAPTER 17

Sources of Encouragement

Who we choose to surround ourselves with will be who we become. Seek out positive people who will build you up rather than tear you down. We all need to hear "I believe in you" during periods in our life. Here are three suggestions on where to look for some of your "I believe in you" people:

1. Consider finding an accountability partner where you can meet in person, virtually (i.e. Skype), and/or through email on a regular basis.

2. Look for positive outside influences to speak into your life such as a coach, a pastor, a councilor, etc.

3. Consider joining or starting your own Mastermind group (see http://www.48day.com for information on how to start one). This is a great way to connect with people seeking similar things in life as you are.

IMPORTANT: Stay away from the negative people and media sources as they will only take you down. Like the old saying goes, one can't fly with the eagles if they are hanging out with the turkeys.

CHAPTER 18
Empowering Attitudes

Positive attitudes will play a large part in your financial success.

There will be periods in your life where you will want to dip into the "Scarlett O'Hara poor me" attitude when life smacks you in the face. This is common, especially when you are going through financial troubles.

The key is to recognize we all have a choice on how we want our attitude to be at all times. There are some people who will choose to live in a "poor me" type of mentality for the rest of their life. Someone or something is always preventing them from being joyful. These people will always remain poor.

You are not one of those people. How can I tell? You made it this far in the book which tells me you are determined to win.

Here are three tips to get your attitude back on track when you hit hard times:

- For every one complaint you have, name three things you are grateful for.

- Quit the sighing and smile even when you don't feel like it.

- Volunteer your time to help out where people are

less fortunate.

Remember, taking action to having a positive attitude is possible. No matter what outside influences happen, it really is possible for everyone to live beyond awesome.

CHAPTER 19
Purposeful Career

Earning money by doing what you love IS possible.

Over half of our population today dislikes their jobs and would change if they could. Wouldn't it be nice to earn more money, work less hours, and do what you love to do? Sound enticing?

Here are four books I recommend for discovering your passion and learning how to transition to the work you love:

1. *No More Dreaded Mondays* by **Dan Miller**

2. *When Wisdom Meets Passion* by **Dan Miller**

3. *Passions ebook* by **Joel and Pei Boggess**

4. *Quitter* by **Jon Acuff**

Remember, it is possible to find passion in the work you do. It just takes intentional **ACTION** towards making it happen.

CHAPTER 20
Job Tips

When one is losing or has lost a job, it is easy to get caught up in panic, worry, and self-doubt. Who could blame a person as there is so much gloom and doom around us.

When looking for a job, remember your emotional state is transparent during job interviews. People are not just looking for the right answers; they are looking for the right person. Body language and how you present yourself are just as important as what you say if not more important.

So what is a person to do when they find themselves in a fearful predicament of needing to find a job?

Here are three easy ways to help convey you are the right person for the job:

1. Be Positive — Consciously stop whining and complaining thoughts from whirling around in your head. Use intentional language to promote positive transformational outcomes (PTO) for yourself. Phrases such as:

   - "I will" (instead of "I should")

   - "I can" (instead of "I wish")

   - "I have" (instead of "if only I had")

2. **Be Confident** — Keep your body language in check. Smile, pull your shoulders back, and walk fast. When you do this, it makes it difficult for one to be down in the dumps. Act confident and you will become bold, courageous, and confident. Remember, someone/someplace is going to be lucky to have you working for them!

3. **Take Care of Yourself** — Be intentional in keeping your emotional energy tank full. Examples include:

   - Exercise

   - Meditate

   - Make time with friends & family, hobbies, etc.

When you keep your emotional tank full, you will be able to keep your "cup overflowing" and in turn give to others while keeping yourself energized.

Being out of work is hard enough without having emotional drainers in your life. You only have a limited amount of time and resources — use them well and avoid negative influences as much as possible.

Remember, success takes intentional action no matter what life throws at you.

CHAPTER 21
Medical Debt Tips

With medical debt being the number one cause of bankruptcy today, it is not unusual for people to find themselves drowning in debt when a medical event hits their lives.

Here are three ways to help patients get their medical debt organized:

Breathe! — Having medical events happen in your life can be stressful enough. Toss on all the extra financial burdens and you are looking at not only additional stress, but also additional health problems stemming off of all this stress. Relax and know that with intentional living, you WILL have your life back in order when you take intentional steps to find solutions.

1. HOW TO HANDLE BILLS — Gather up all your medical related statements including the Explanation of Benefit (EOB) forms sent from your insurance company as well as your medical bills and put them in ONE place. Go through them and:

2. Keep ONLY the current bill for each provider. Toss out any redundant old copies.

   • Match up EACH Explanation of Benefit statement (EOB) to each medical bill.

- Highlight the PATIENT RESPONSIBILITY portion on each EOB and ensure that corresponds with your medical bill. Ensure that your medical bill and EOB match up. If they do not, contact your insurance company for assistance.

- List each medical debt into your debt snowball and list it from smallest to largest.

- IMPORTANT: BE PROACTIVE AND CONTACT YOUR MEDICAL PROVIDER'S BILLING OFFICE DIRECTLY TO SET UP A PAYMENT PLAN (DO NOT WAIT FOR THEM TO CONTACT YOU).

  I. By contacting the billing office directly, you are showing yourself to be a person who is taking intentional steps in paying your bill which they appreciate.

  II. Ask to be set up on a regular monthly payment plan that will fit into your budget.

  III. If you are unable to set up a payment plan within your budget, do NOT over promise what you cannot afford. Instead, ask to speak to the head of the organization. If that doesn't work, continue to send what regular payments you can afford.

    - Hospitals and clinics are usually willing to work with you on a payment plan. If you are unable to get help, let them know you will be transferring care.

    - NOTE: If you know you will have large amounts of out of pocket expenses ahead of time, be proactive in working with their billing department ahead of time. Some places will offer upfront discounts for patients who are paying out of pocket.

3. HOW TO HANDLE LARGE OUT OF POCKET EXPENSES — If you have an extraordinarily large amount of out of pocket expenses that are going to take you years to pay off, consider the following:

- Contact the medical administrator leader for the healthcare provider that is billing you (preferably in person, however, if not an option, at least by phone and/or letter).

I. Express gratitude for the care you have received and explain your goal is to pay every penny back.

II. Have your written budget ready to reference – this will help answer any questions and show that you are being intentional in paying off your debt.

III. Ask if they would be willing to write off some of the medical expenses and set you up on monthly payment plan that fits into your budget.

IV. Depending on your situation, consider requesting a deeper discount if you are able to get a loan from your local bank or credit union to pay the debt in full and at the same time have the loan be in payments that fit your budget. DISCLAIMER: While I do NOT endorse taking out loans to incur more debt, I do find that in certain circumstances it IS okay to transfer the debt to someone else as long as you know that this doesn't give you the freedom to use that loan to spend on other things.

- If working with a hospital facility, contact them to see if they have a patient advocate/social worker type person that can provide you with additional resources.

CHAPTER 22
Problem-Solving Tips

Making excuses is a convenient copout for staying in a 'poor me' mentality state of life. There is ALWAYS a "but, I can't because..." type excuse waiting to be used for all of us.

If you are continuously making excuses about your situation, my advice is to "STOP!"

Why is this so important?

- Ditching the constant use of excuses and instead finding solutions WILL propel you into becoming victorious.

- Continuously seeking out solutions will get you to your financial goals whereas excuses will keep you trapped in muck.

The ICAN problem-solving method is a great tool for getting you started how to continuously problem-solve. After a while, the ICAN™ problem-solving method will become second nature:

Issue: Identify the ISSUE — What is the problem? Is this problem a symptom of a much bigger problem that I need to address?

Cause: Identify the CAUSE — Why is this issue happening? How can I take personal responsibility?

Answer: Identify the ANSWER — What are possible solutions? How can I find creative out of the box solutions versus just looking at the obvious?

NO Excuses: Simple, **NO excuses** — How can I stop myself from making excuses? What action steps can I take instead?

Two awesome books I recommend on learning the power of taking personal responsibility are:

QBQ! The Question Behind the Question by John G. Miller

Flipping the Switch: Unleash the Power of Personal Accountability Using the QBQ! by John G. Miller

CHAPTER 23
Taking Action is Key

It is one thing to dream of becoming rich, but it is quite another to take action to become rich.

My best advice to you on taking action to achieve financial success is:

- "MOVE IT." Don't wait for perfection, just start now.

- Learn from the best and then put this education to use in your own life.

- Forgive and keep moving when you goof up.

Becoming debt free and living an abundant life is possible. However, if you are sitting around waiting to become rich, it isn't going to happen. Intentional action is required.

Here are three steps to take in getting your finances in order:

- Put a stake in the ground and take action to put together a budget.

- Say enough is enough and take action each day to live on a written budget.

- Take action to get back on your budget no matter how many times you goof up.

Three things to keep in mind as you take action to change your finances:

- Remember, no one is born knowing master personal finances so be patient with yourself.

- You are never going to have a perfect month, so get over it.

- You are going to do **AWESOME** when you take action. **REMEMBER:** The key to achieving awesomeness starts with **ABC** (Action Bring Change).

YOUR AWESOME NOTES

YOUR AWESOME NOTES

YOUR AWESOME NOTES

YOUR AWESOME NOTES

YOUR AWESOME NOTES

YOUR AWESOME NOTES

YOUR AWESOME NOTES

YOUR AWESOME NOTES

ACKNOWLEDGEMENTS

Dave Ramsey and Staff – THANK you for your ministry. The stuff you guys doing is LIFE changing stuff! You have shown us that the impossible IS possible when it comes to gaining financial peace in our lives.

Dan Miller – THANK YOU for mentoring me into discovering my passion, purpose, and dreams as well as for your kindness and friendship.

Kent Julian – THANK YOU for coaching me how to become one heck of a speaker and for your friendship.

My 48Days.Net Friends & Mentors – You guys just plain ROCK! You are a constant source of synergy, encouragement, and just plain FUN!

Joshua Brown & Frances Copeland – Thank you both for your wonderful eyes for details, your time, and your kindness!

Jacob Walgrave – Thank you for sharing your incredible talent of editing – you have a wonderful gift!

Trish Englund – Thank you for sharing your editing talent on yet another book! I love how you don't even miss a beat when you get the midnight email asking for your advice, wisdom and input on a new project.

Pei Boggess, Kathleen Crandall, Jane Mueller, and Ann Musico – Thank you each for your 6am morning motivation calls throughout this journey! Your friendships are a blessing in my life!

Mom – Well it goes without saying, I want to thank you for being an awesome role model and the best mom in the world. I love you and I am SO PROUD of you! You inspire and motivate not only me, but our whole family. You truly do live beyond awesome!

Remy – Keep on questioning the status quo my feisty child – it will help you grow into the brilliant person you are meant to be. I can't wait to see you light the world on fire with your passion and purpose. You are persistent, a charmer, and incredibly smart.

Max – Keep pursuing ways to take action on your dreams – you have such a magnificent aurora about you. I see such great things about you Max – you are a deep thinker who will courageously blaze trails for others to follow. You are courageous, brilliant and wonderful!

Robbie – Keep exploring areas to grow and learn – you have such a gift for being a fountain of information. Others will be blessed by your focused intensity – you are going to gift the world with your talents and skills. You are intelligent, kind, and brave.

Maggie – Keep seeking out areas where your gifts and passions live - you have such a gift for bringing out the best in others. Your amazing gifts of kindness and generosity are going to pave wide and deep trails in this world kiddo. You are wise, confident, and adventurous.

Bobby – Ahhh…Eggs, my best friend. I love you so much kiddo and am so blessed get to be married to my "favorite husband in the world." Your unwavering patience, kindness and support have meant the world to me. Thanks for reminding me to have fun in life, for the adventures throughout the years, and for the adventures yet to come!

God — Thank you for every lesson and every blessing!

Connect With Jen

Jen McDonough lives in Lindstrom, Minnesota with her handsome husband, four awesome kids, two dogs, and one ugly mortgage.

She is an ordinary person living an extraordinary life. As an engaging speaker, author, and coach, she demonstrates to her audiences that taking intentional ACTION leads organizations and individuals to success.

Audiences connect with her authenticity as she shares real life stories that are filled with humor, fear, pain, embarrassment, success, faith, joy, hope, inspiration, and positive transformational outcomes (PTO's).

Jen is the accomplished Amazon Top 100 author of *Living Beyond Awesome, Living Beyond Rich,* and *5 Minutes a Day to Living Beyond Rich.*

You can connect with Jen on her weekly live shows which also air on Sticher and Itunes (The Iron Jen Show), through her weekly website blogs, on Twitter, Facebook, and through her website (www.TheIronJen.com).

Interested in having Jen speak at your next event? Visit her website at www.TheIronJen.com and click on her speaking page to check her availability.

Remember, if she can do it, YOU can do it! Take action today to live extraordinary tomorrow.

Connect with Jen:

Website: www.TheIronJen.com
Twitter: @TheIronJen
LinkedIn: JenMcDonough
Facebook: The Iron Jen